HANS NIELSEN HAUGE

HAUGEANISM

A BRIEF SKETCH OF THE
MOVEMENT AND SOME
OF ITS CHIEF EXPONENTS

BY

M. O. WEE

WIPF & STOCK · Eugene, Oregon

Wipf and Stock Publishers
199 W 8th Ave, Suite 3
Eugene, OR 97401

Haugeanism
A Brief Sketch of the Movement and
Some of its Chief Exponents
By Wee, M. O.
ISBN 13: 978-1-55635-647-6
ISBN 10: 1-55635-647-1
Publication date 10/2/2007
Previously published by M. O. Wee, 1919

PREFACE

My first impressions of Haugeanism I received from father and mother.

From them I learned to respect the Haugeans, and to cherish the principles of the movement. For that reason I think it is fitting that I should dedicate these pages to them.

On the other hand I desire to express my gratitude to Arthur Rholl, Rev. H. N. Bakke and Prof. Herman E. Jorgenson for valuable suggestions and assistance in translating, and to Dr. O. M. Norlie because he was so kind as to write the introduction, besides also assisting otherwise.

In writing, I have especially had the young people of our dear Lutheran Church in mind. For I am decidedly of the opinion that a better knowledge of the lives and labors of worthy men and women of our Church will make them more fit for their own high calling. If this little book should in some measure bring this about, my purpose is accomplished.

Luther Seminary, St. Paul, Minn., January, 1919.
THE AUTHOR.

"Lat os inkje forfederne gløyma
under alt som me venda og snu!
For dei gav os ein arv til aa gøyma.
Han er større enn mange vil tru."
—Ivar Aasen.

CONTENTS

AT MOTHER'S GRAVE

"Hun lærte mig hun, før hun sa et ord:
Det største som Gud kan give,
er ikke at bli berømt og stor,
men menneske sandt at blive."

INTRODUCTION

The scene is an old-fashioned local grist mill near Nærø, Norway. The persons in the story are one Ole, called "Læsar" or "Reader", because he read his Bible and devotional books with zeal, and another named Andreas, who was just a plain man of the world, a member in good standing in the Church, but not in any way "peculiar", in the sense that Christians should be peculiar people (Peter 2:9). Now, at the mill the good rule, "first come, first served", was observed. Ole did come first, arriving at the mill before nightfall; but he spent some time in his boat reading, and Andreas took advantage of this fact and got his sack to the mill first. Ole did not get angry, but sat down quietly, waiting the whole night for Andreas's job to be completed. For Andreas, this turned out to be the most significant night in his life, because then the first principles of the right use of the Word of God was laid up in his heart, and that by a man who in ridicule was called "a Bible Reader". While sitting around and waiting for the corn to be ground, Ole began in meekness a conversation with Andreas, whose meaning he did not then at all understand, but which later became of vast importance to him. Andreas had a good historical knowledge of the way of salvation, but he had no living faith in Christ, and therefore he continued to live according to the worldly standards of his time and place.

It would be worth while here to record the whole conversation as carried on between these two men, all alone during the long hours of watching at the mill; but we do not have space for the whole story. Ole began talking about the wonderful way in which the stones made corn into meal. Andreas could not see anything wonderful about that. Ole thought that it was possible to see in the mill God's deep purpose as to created things. Andreas thought that was plain enough, but still not at all wonderful. Ole proceeded to say that since man was the highest visible creation, he must have been created for the highest office. Andreas assented to this without thinking anything more about it at the time; but Ole did not feel satisfied with Andreas's disinterest. He took up the matter of creation again, and Andreas admitted that everything had been created very good and also for a purpose, and even that all the created things were intended to serve man. "But, whom should man serve?" asked Ole. The question was unexpected. It was penetrating. Andreas had been told that the "Readers" did not think, but just read, sang, prayed, felt and sacrificed. But Andreas was not going to be silenced, so he answered with a bold front, "God, of course." Ole then asked, "Is it still true that we all should serve Him?" To this Andreas answered, "Yes", without knowing what such service meant. Then Ole, knowing full well that Andreas did not understand what he was saying, began to explain that he himself had not understood what these words meant before he was awakened. He had, indeed, lived a respectable life, as judged by the world, and even by the average church member. He used to swear a little, liked to play cards, went to dances, got drunk once in a while, and the like. He never prayed from his heart. He did not attend services to serve the Lord, but he was accounted to be as good as anybody else — neither better nor worse, in short, a pretty good fellow. But deep down in his heart he was not happy, and when the awakening came to him he saw the sinfulness of his ways, the deep depravity of his heart, and his lost condition.

While Ole was speaking, the mill stopped. Everything in the mill became silent, except the monotonous noise of the water. The night was dark. In this stillness Andreas's thoughts turned to his own condition, and he became sensible of an unrest, which at that time he did not understand, nor did he then understand the fact that the Holy Spirit calls sinners to repentance and faith through instruments and means. As the mill had stopped, they both went out to search for the cause. The mill was built in such a way that it was turned by a large water wheel. The water came to the wheel through a shoot. This was placed several feet above the earth so that one had to use a ladder to reach it. Andreas climbed up the ladder and discovered what had made the mill stop. The water had carried a large piece of sod, which had choked up the spout so that the water ran off to both sides. Ole, standing below, asked what the trouble was. Andreas had gotten respect for him, for he perceived that he spoke the truth. But a bad habit is not easily cast aside, so when he answered, he tried, as was his custom, to make his words emphatic by an oath. But as soon as the oath left his mouth, it struck him that it was a shame to swear in Ole's hearing. On account of the murmuring of the waterfall, Ole had not heard the answer, and asked again what the matter was. This time Andreas simply answered that it was only a large piece of sod that had filled the shoot. He did not think then of the fact that he was more afraid of this poor man than he was of the All-knowing and Almighty God.

After the sod had been removed, the mill wheel turned again and the men went inside to continue their discourse about eternal values. They spoke about many things. Andreas began to open up his heart and to ask questions. They spoke about the meaning of service, of the new birth, of the prodigal life and the life of sonship, of communion with God, of the Means of Grace, of sin and salvation, of pardon and assurance, and the like. Every time that Ole cited a Bible passage, Andreas remembered having seen it or heard it at some time, and it became clear to him that Ole's story was true. But it puzzled him why he had not understood it before, and why the pastor had not explained these things to him. Towards dawn Ole sang a hymn of renunciation. Andreas's thoughts were carried to the churchyard, to his mother's grave. Again he lived through his childhood days when mother had sat at the wheel and spun, and he had sat at her side and read in the Bible, and was praised by her when he had read well. "Mother was surely born again," thought he, "and now she is with Jesus in glory." While he sat, musing thus, Ole gave him his hand and said farewell.

This was the beginning of Andreas's awakening and his transformation from being the servant of the Devil to being an ambassador in Christ's stead. Andreas is not mentioned by Prof. Wee in the following account. We do not either mean to say that he should have been mentioned as one of the notable followers of Hans Nielsen Hauge. We do not even want to state his full name, although he spent thirteen years of work in the Lord's service as a consecrated, awakened layman, and over forty years in the Gospel ministry. A minister, one of the many young men who through his influence became pastors, says that he was earnest and inspiring, original and practical, zealous that the truth should be spoken without respect of person, that all might be awakened to a living faith, and to be preserved in this faith — in short, that he was a soul winner of the most practical and consecrated type, being, like Ole at the grist mill, always ready to put in a good word for his Master, and to give a good account of the hope that was within him.

*   *   *

REV. A. WRIGHT
Referred to in this introduction

The reason why we have told at such length the story of Ole and Andreas at the mill, is, that it illustrates the spirit and workings of Haugeanism. Now, some say that Haugeanism is dead, admitting that it was a movement which truly brought a great number of blessings to Norway a century ago, but maintaining that it belonged only to that time and place, and that it can in no wise apply to our own country and our own times. And, indeed, it must be admitted as a historical fact that Haugeanism did bring to Norway many blessings. It brought a great spiritual awakening which penetrated deep down into the lowest classes of society, and far up into the highest professorships at the University. This spiritual awakening was closely followed by an awakening in other lines — national and political, industrial and intellectual. In fact, every department of thought and endeavor felt the throb and inspiration of the new spiritual life. Hans Nielsen Hauge died in 1824, but he left hundreds and thousands of inspired men and women who continued the good work which he had begun. In 1825 the Norwegian emigration to America began, and Haugeanism was transplanted to this country by thousands of faithful followers of Hauge.

*   *   *

The powers and the activities of the human soul may be divided into three classes: feeling, knowing and willing. In some people the feelings are apt to be strong, in others the intellect, and in a third class the will; while in the fourth class, all these activities are equally strong. With respect to religion, the emotional type of mind is apt to lay special stress on the emotional side of religion, the intellectual type of mind, on the intellectual side of religion, and the volition type of mind, on the practical side of religion; while the balanced mind would emphasize every phase of religion. We also find that we have emotional types of religious movements, intellectual types and volitional types, as well as movements which combine the three in perfect harmony.

A very strong emotional type leads to a disregard for creeds and forms, and a great emphasis on personal experience and personal witnessing, speaking with tongues, and extreme subjectivism, sentimentalism and ecstasy in worship. The emotional type of worship may be illustrated by the various schools of mystics, the "Free Free" and most of the modern revivals.

The intellectual type lays strong emphasis on an educated ministry and scholarly sermons, on stately liturgies, on doctrines and forms. The self-righteous Pharisees and the learned scribes belong to this class. It is well known that the Greek church calls herself the Orthodox Church above all others, but it is the most stagnant. The Roman Catholic Church has laid much stress on the intellectual side, but its history is also one of the greatest opposition to the Gospel of Jesus Christ and of the most intolerant and cruel persecutions of the true believers. The Protestant rationalists of the eighteenth century and the negative "higher critics" of our day are alike deadly enemies of true Christianity.

A very strong volitional type lays stress on action and practical results, often utterly disregarding the principles which should guide the actions and be the basis of the results. The course of action followed, may be on the one hand a complete withdrawal from the world, such as the old ascetics and monks practised. The course of action may, on the other hand, be such as the modern social service advocates practise. They are busy about everything under the sun, but mostly about things which do not belong to the sphere of church activities. The Church is called to preach the Word in its truth and purity, and to administer the Sacraments rightly, calling upon all lost and condemned sinners to repent and believe and to walk in the newness of life. The social service advocates often do not know a whit about the Bible, and openly declare that they can not conduct charities by parading Christ. They are concerned about conventions, campaigns, drives, schemes, methods, reforms and moral uplift through personal effort, in doing good for practical reasons. At times they advocate that all the Churches be consolidated into one organization that shall have no creed, that shall include everybody in a certain town or place, without regard to his personal relation to Christ, that this organization shall have a swimming pool, a committee on charities, an insurance agent, a good preacher who shall belong to no Denomination and shall be satisfactory to all, a business expert to guide the business men of the town, an agricultural expert to instruct the farmers, a physical director and a movie operator, and the like.

As we look at the various extreme tendencies in religious life, it occurs to us that they are in a way similar to the lack of mental balance of the insane. Many of the symptoms of insanity are only exaggerated forms of the ordinary mental processes. A person may be perfectly sound in every way excepting one. For example, it may be that his emotional powers are disturbed. He may be, on the one hand, too easily and strongly excited or depressed; or he may, on the other hand, show absolutely no feeling or interest whatever in what goes on about him. Meanwhile, his intellect and will may be in good working order. Another unfortunate has a deranged intellect. He can not learn to read and write. He can not remember at all, and, of course, he can not reason. Or, perhaps he goes to the other extreme, and is a maniac as to one pet subject or one freak idea. A third case before us is one who exhibits a continual press of activities, flying from one task to another, changing from one topic of conversation to another, without much, if any, logical connection. Finally, there are also those who are helplessly and hopelessly deficient in all the mental capacities—emotional, intellectual and volitional.

It must not be understood that the religious types which we have mentioned are here characterized as types of insanity. We mention them only as an illustration of unbalanced minds; and with this respect, the insane are to some extent like the unbalanced sane. To emphasize only the feelings in religion, or the doctrines, or church activities, is, to say the least, not a mark of religious balance. Christian faith is more than a state of feeling, or an assent of the intellect, or a motion of the will. It is all of these — uniting our whole person with the life of Christ.

Religion is essentially emotional. It calls for such emotions as fear, love, hope, joy, sorrow, shame, remorse and peace. It calls into play the finest affections, the highest desires and deepest sentiments. The feelings are motives to human action, but they should not run riot.

Religion is also essentially intellectual. There can be no strong Christian life without a good knowledge of the main facts of God's Word relating to sin and grace — especially to Christ as the only Savior from sin, death and the power of the Devil. We do not wonder, then, that some Church Bodies lay such great stress on the instruction of the young and the value of creed. We can also understand that in the struggle and confusion of this world they may forget all the other essentials, excepting this one, and finally they become unbalanced and degenerate into a cold, intolerant, rationalistic and stagnant sect. It must not be forgotten that faith precedes understanding, that knowledge alone is not religion, that God chose the foolish things of the world to confound the wise; and that the crucified Christ was unto the learned Jews a stumbling block and unto the wise Greeks foolishness.

Religion is also essentially action, that is, moral action in accordance with the will of God. Our first parents were commanded to obey. The Moral Law expressed in our conscience and revealed on Mt. Sinai tells us what to do and what not to do. The Gospel of the New Covenant requires that we shall believe in the Triune God and walk in the footsteps of Jesus. Our will is everywhere called into action to choose and to carry out the command of the Lord. "Choose ye this day whom ye will serve" (Joshua 24:15). "Not everyone that saith unto Me: 'Lord, Lord', shall enter into the Kingdom of Heaven, but he that doeth the will of My Father, Which is in Heaven" (Matt. 7:21). "If a man shall do His will he shall know of the doctrine whether it be of God or whether I speak of Myself" (John 7:17). "He that saith, I know Him and keepeth not His commands is a liar, and the truth is not in him" (John 2:4). We are thus required by Holy Writ not only to do certain things, but also not to do certain things. We must not only say, "I will," but also "I won't," as Joseph said: "How, then, can I do this great wickedness and sin against God?" (Gen. 39:9). We must not only love the Lord and know His will, but we must obey Him. Works without faith are dead and cannot save us, but faith without works is also dead (James 2:24).

It is therefore plain that the Christian religion is essentially emotional, intellectual and volitional. It quickens our sensibilities. It enlightens our understanding. It commands our will to direct all our energies according to God's Word. It demands nothing short of the best that is in us, it makes use of every capacity and power of the human soul. Since Christianity involves every feeling, every faculty of the intellect and the whole will, it is able to make us new creatures in Christ, so that we can grow into the measure of the stature of the fullness of Christ (Eph. 4:13). Therefore, the religious life that we live should not be unbalanced either towards the emotional states or the intellectual or the volitional, but should include all of these three in happy combination.

As one looks out upon the world he becomes at once aware of a terrible confusion of religious sects and many religious movements within each Church Body. There are so few Denominations which seem to lay equal stress on the different essential parts of religion. Most of them are unbalanced in one way or another, and so it is also with the religious movements. They run to one extreme or to another. Blessed is the age, the land and the Church that experience the healthy workings of a balanced religious movement, or that number Christians whose religious character has been harmoniously developed.

*   *   *

When we examine the Haugean movement in the Norwegian Church we are almost at once struck by the fact that it was a balanced movement. The emotional, intellectual and volitional sides of religion were all emphasized by Hans Nielsen Hauge and his most representative followers. It is for that reason that Haugeanism was of such great, such varied and such lasting blessing to Norway. It is for this reason that we feel assured that Haugeanism does belong to our place and time. We have had a number of Haugeans amongst us in this country for years back. Some of them were found in the so-called Hauge Synod, but many members of that body were by no means typical Haugeans. Some of them were also found in other Norwegian Lutheran Synods, even though they did not go by the name of Haugeans. There are Christians of the Haugean mind and character also in other Denominations who have in no way been influenced either directly or indirectly by the Haugeanism of Norway. The Haugeanism of Norway did not really begin with Hans Nielsen Hauge a century ago. The full and free and well balanced Christian life typical of Haugeanism is pictured in the Bible itself, and has found many worthy representatives down through the ages, both in Bible and secular times. The Norwegian type of well balanced and vigorous Christianity called Haugeanism, is, however, of special concern to us, because it is part of our history and has, therefore, a special appeal to us and should make a profound impression on our people when they really begin to understand it. This book on Haugeanism by Prof. M. O. Wee seeks to explain what the movement was, and gives brief sketches of some of the leading Haugeans in the Old Country and in this country. This little book has a mission. It is our sincerest hope and prayer that it will help many to attain to a fuller, stronger and more balanced religious life.

—O. M. NORLIE.

HAUGEANISM

*A Brief Sketch of the Movement and Some of Its
Chief Exponents*

I. HAUGEANS

The Haugeans represent a spiritual movement,
and are not to be considered as a sect or a party.
Certain fundamental principles are essential to the
movement which they inaugurated. Such principles
are always only partly understood and appropriated,
and sometimes they are misunderstood and even mis-
construed. Besides, in this as in every other movement, such fundamental principles are seldom given
the opportunity for unhindered development.

Every spiritual movement is represented to the
best advantage by those of its exponents who have
grasped the movement in its essentials, although even
these are never capable of representing it in its en-
tirety. A spiritual movement does not arise fulfledged;
it develops gradually and organically in accordance
with its laws. And yet God-sent prophets within any
such movement live not only in their own times, but
also in many respects ahead of their times. They are
as a rule better representatives of a movement than
their first disciples, especially with respect to compre-
hensiveness. It is, therefore, impossible to discuss

such a movement without a somewhat intimate knowledge of its founders and most prominent exponents. For our purpose it will be sufficient to discuss two of these within Haugeanism, namely, the founder of the movement, the layman Hans Nielsen Hauge; and its greatest representative among the learned of the Church of Norway, Prof. Gisle Johnson; and in addition, a few of the more prominent of their immediate followers.

Hans Nielsen Hauge

Although books have been written and could still be written about Hans Nielsen Hauge, we must necessarily be brief and confine ourselves to a few of the essentials. Edv. Sverdrup says in his work "Fra Norges Kristenliv": "He (Hauge) became. viewed in a general way, the chosen and commissioned instrument of God to lead our people out of the night of unenlightenment and forth into a new life in the light of God's Word. Therefore, in writing the history of the Church of modern Norway, chief mention must be made of Hauge and of that awakening which originated with him. And it is altogether impossible to write the history of inner missions in our land without basing it upon that man and that awakening which constitute the living source of all voluntary Christian work in Norway. Through the work and the suffering of Hauge, lay preaching was established in the Christian life of Norway with such power and with such evident results that it could not again be smothered. This was due to the fact that hand in hand with the newly-awakened life came also the full realization of the obligation of Christian witnessing.

And with the newly-awakened life followed also the gift of testimony which was necessary to sustain it and to transmit it to others . . . That Hauge's life-work was not nullified, but became the source of so rich a display of the powers of Christian life, was a result of the fact that among Hauge's friends and immediate followers there arose a deep consciousness of spiritual independence due to confidence in God and in a cause which they felt was from Him. This sense of independence could, it is true, for a time be held in abeyance by the burdens of tribulation, but not destroyed. On the contrary, these burdens rather steeled and strengthened it. And this sense of spiritual independence which grew up among Hauge's friends was destined to have far-reaching consequences. It was not only that this made of Hauge's friends the best of citizens and of many of them the most prominent leaders in the various walks of life, nor that through them there was planted a seed of freedom in the development of our whole national life; but, above all, through the vitality and sense of independence in the awakening by Hauge — created and nourished by the Spirit and Word of God — there was made a permanently vital contribution to the spiritual life of our people, affirming the freedom and right of conscience, awakening zeal for salvation of souls, and calling into use the gifts of grace."

Hauge is described as a quiet and meditative personality from childhood on. From his mother he learned hymns and prayers, and the father usually, at the close of day, gathered the family for worship. He was by nature deeply religious and early in life meditated on religious problems. Games and merry-making held no interest for him. Even in his youth, sorrow over sin and the vanities of the world, and the question of how to be saved, were his only concern. At an early age it was found to be expedient for him to leave his home in order, through hard work, to provide a livelihood. He sought to harmonize, in his thoughts as well as in his life, the spiritual and the material interests — at first with very little success.

Then, on that memorable April day, in 1796, came his awakening, and with it the divine call to witness for his Savior. The call was, apparently, direct. "It burned within him, so that he could not keep silent." His first concern was for his own — father, mother, sisters and brothers —; thereafter for his countrymen, even to the furthermost corners of Norway. He was, however, often filled with anxiety, even unto tears, at the thought of the great task and the heavy responsibility, yea, he even pleaded with God to relieve him of the pressing duty and rather send forth a bishop or some other prominent man. But the call never released him until his life's sun set.

The path of sorrow which fell to the lot of Hauge because of his call to preach the Gospel, is now quite generally known. He was branded as an idler (løsgjænger) and a tramp (landstryker). To dispose of such as these there was the so-called court of the house of correction (tugthusret)— in the country, the county judge (sorenskriver), in the city, the town judge (byfogd). No "idler" was granted counsel for defense in order that, as it was explained, "justice might not be unnecessarily delayed through parleyings and technicalities." The decision could not be appealed; the invariable verdict was, if guilty, detention in the house of correction. The term of imprisonment was decided by the commission for the poor, which consisted of the pastor, elders, and two men appointed by the sheriff. "This is what the apparatus looked like, which exercised control over the itinerant lay preachers."

Hauge's view of afflictions and persecutions was, that one should to the uttermost exercise humility and longsuffering and reward evil with good. In spite of all persecutions from the clergy, Hauge stood unequivocally by his church, and in spite of the most unjust treatment from civil authorities, one will hunt in vain for a single word of disloyalty from Hauge, by mouth or pen. Hauge was not alone in being subjected to such unfair treatment. In 1799 no less than six lay preachers of the Hauge movement were committed to the Kristiania House of Correction "for vagrancy and desire to preach (prædikelyst)", two of whom were detained there about two years and six months. One of these was Hauge's own brother, Mikkel Hauge.

But Hauge was also a man of a highly practical bent. Concerning this we quote from "Nordmænd i det nittende aarhundrede": "In the country district called Maalselven, the opinion had become current among the awakened (vakte) that in order to be a real earnest Christian one must cease from all manual labor.

"On one of his tours Hauge came to this district, and when it was rumored that he had come, a great number of people gathered at the place where he stayed, expecting as a matter of course that he at once would hold a meeting. But Hauge had walked over to a waterfall nearby to investigate whether or not it could be used for some industrial purpose. When those assembled heard that the stranger occupied him-

self with things of so worldly a nature, they were
immediately convinced that this man could not be
Hauge, but must be some pretender posing as the
renowned man of God and now seeking to pull the
wool over their eyes. This suspicion was confirmed
when Hauge returned, and, seeing them, bluntly told
them to go to work; that loafing was unjustified in
such favorable weather. With that he lent a hand
himself and aided in the work until evening. Then
he asked them to gather, and thereupon spoke to them
in such a way that no one could doubt that it was
Hauge himself who had come to them. And this in-
cident gave them to understand that it was possible
to be an earnest Christian, and yet, at the same time,
an industrious and efficient laborer."

"It was impossible for Hauge to be idle; if he was
not occupied with anything else, he knitted or
mended his clothes." Hauge established, as is well
known, a paper mill, a stamping mill, a bone mill, a
flour mill, a tannery, yes, even a foundry for church
bells and small cannon.

"Furthermore, there was about Hauge a singularly
sound and genuine human way of dealing with men
and affairs. On several occasions, a vein of humor—
genuine peasant humor, peculiar to eastern Norway—
comes to light." Many interesting incidents from his
life testify to this, but lack of space prevents us from
relating further. It may be stated that Hans Nielsen
Hauge was typically Norwegian. Therefore Grundtvig rightly said that through Hauge the national spirit
of Norway was awakened.

Thus, briefly sketched, that man appears who became the founder and standard bearer of Haugeanism.
And the influence he exercised over his friends was

deep and lasting. Like Hauge, most of his friends were efficient and industrious workers in city and country districts. "It is touching to read of these old lay preachers, how, without pay, they travelled afoot over mountain and vale to encourage their brethren and to rouse the spiritually sleeping. The sword of the law threatened them, and a zealous clergy ever sought opportunity to bring it into use. Many suffered imprisonment, all were subjected to derision and indignities of all kinds. But in those very times the Norwegian lay preachers were endowel with a power of spirit and of faith, and a willing consecration to the service of God as never before." [1] "At an earlier time it would have been something unusual if anyone, born a peasant, had become anything but a peasant, but now many a peasant among the Haugeans came to the cities, perhaps to found a mercantile establishment, or to learn a trade, or to open a factory or start some other industrial enterprise. . . . A new spirit, a power and energy hitherto unknown, was created in Norway." [2]

John Haugvaldstad

Of the numerous lay preachers that the awakening through Hauge called forth, John Haugvaldstad probably is unequaled. Like Hauge, Haugvaldstad was by nature quiet and introspective. He, too, for several years pondered over religious questions. For many years his restless soul sought peace with God, seemingly without avail. One Sunday morning, after a prolonged illness, he was reading a devotional book. The following words caught his eye: "Thou who sit-

1. Skagestads "Lægmandsbevægelsen i Norge."
2. "Nordmænd i det 19de aarhundrede."

test on high, and yet beholdest with compassion the
lowly, look upon us miserable ones, we pray Thee,
from Thy high Heaven." These words brought hope
and new light to his despondent heart. Not until 1801

JOHN HAUGVALDSTAD

did Hauge pay a visit to the farm, Haugvaldstad, and
through personal contact and conversation with this
man of God, he found peace of soul. Not long after
this he began publicly to confess his faith in Christ.
He made several extended journeys—covering prac-

tically all of Norway. While Hauge was in prison,
many of his followers were intimidated by the attitude of the civil authorities and ceased preaching; not
so with Haugvaldstad. Three times he visited with
the brethren in Denmark; three times he went to
Sweden for the same purpose; and once he made a
trip to Germany, mainly to become acquainted with
the work for foreign missions. "Enriched through the
information which he had gathered and with increased
courage, he went home and gave the impetus to the
founding of "Det Norske Missionsselskab", founded
in Stavanger, 1842." "Haugvaldstad is the first in the
Church of Norway to awaken a more general interest
for missions."

In 1845 a chapel (bedehus) was erected in Stavanger, mainly through his efforts. In this chapel religious meetings were held every Sunday evening, besides mid-week meetings. Whenever regular services were held in the churches, the old Haugeans
never held meetings of their own. The form of service at their meetings was very simple. It opened
with the singing of a hymn suitable for the day.
Thereupon one of the younger Christians would offer
a free prayer. At the Sunday meetings this was followed by the reading of a sermon on the Gospel or
Epistle for the day. These selections were from the
postils of Luther, Henrik Müller, Jesper Brockman,
or from "Samlingspostillen", published by H. N.
Hauge. At the mid-week gatherings selections were
read from Christian Scriver's "Sjæleskat", Johan
Arndt's "Sande Kristendom," or some other good book
recommended for that purpose. Song and prayer pre-
ceded and followed the reading. Then Haugvaldstad
or one of the older Christians would speak briefly,

admonishing the hearers. If there was a visiting and
well known layman present, he was asked to speak
either in connection with what had been read, or from
his own experience. At times the preaching was
based on some part of the Catechism or the unabridged
Explanation.

Haugvaldstad sought in his speaking not so much
to stir the emotions as to arouse the conscience and
urge the will to decision. "The quintessence of his
message was an urgent appeal to acknowledge one's
sin, to turn to God, to believe in the crucified and
resurrected Savior, Jesus Christ, and to follow Him
in a holy life."

"Haugvaldstad was a man of few words. He was
very careful and slow to arrive at decisions, but firm
and persevering in carrying them out. He stood firm
as a rock upon acknowledged truth, not changing in
spite of the varied opinions of others. Through the
trials and tribulations of life — not the least in his
own home — he developed into a harmonious Christian character, always maintaining his poise, and he
always had a word of wisdom or advice to offer to
others." By the grace of God he was instrumental in
uniting the Christians, and in love maintaining the
spirit of peace and harmony. The boys of his home
town called him "Holy John", and even his enemies
said concerning him: "If anyone is a Christian, it is
John Haugvaldstad."

On New Year's Eve, 1850, while taking a personal
gift of 560 crowns ($150) to the Jewish mission, he
was struck with paralysis, from which he died the
same day. The funeral services were held at the
Stavanger cathedral. The great multitude present
bore witness to the high esteem in which he was held

in his community. All places of business were closed. As he, while he lived had remembered the poor and the needy, as, for instance, he had founded the Josephine orphanage, and had given large sums to missions, so, at his death, he willed his whole estate to like purposes. Haugvaldstad must, without question, be numbered among the prominent men of Norway.

Elling Eielsen

A Haugean who was destined to take a very important part in church work here in America, was Elling Eielsen. Born at Voss, Norway, in 1804, he was born again in 1832, and soon afterwards began to preach—at first in Maalselven and Bardo, later in Trondhjem and the southern part of Norway. He made trips to Sweden and also to Denmark,

ELLING EIELSEN

where he was put in jail for conducting religious meetings.

In 1839 he came to America, where he went about preaching, especially in Illinois and Wisconsin. He was ordained in 1843 by Rev. F. A. Hofman, a German Lutheran pastor, and thus became the first Norwegian Lutheran pastor in America. He was a tireless worker and made many and far-reaching trips in the interest of home missions, in Illinois, Wisconsin, Minnesota, South Dakota and Texas—always going on foot.

In 1846 he directed the organization of "The Evangelical Lutheran Church in America", which body in

1876 changed its name to "Hauge's Norwegian Evangelical Lutheran Synod in America."

Mr. Eielsen, in 1842, caused the publication of Pontoppidan's Explanation and the Augsburg Confession. These books were the first Norwegian books to be printed in this country. To bring about this, he walked from Chicago to New York, a distance of about one thousand miles. Of even greater interest to many of our readers is perhaps the fact that Mr. Eielsen already in 1841 had Luther's Smaller Catechism translated and published in English by a New York firm. When traveling he often slept outdoors. Carrying on his shoulders a knapsack, which contained some necessities, such as an axe, a coffee pot, cup and plate, etc., he tramped over the most desolate regions in search of his countrymen, in order to bring them the Bread of Life.

Eielsen passed away in Chicago January 10th, 1883, at the age of 78. He had then been in constant service as a preacher for more than fifty years. Directly, and to a still greater extent indirectly, the influence of the industrious life of Elling Eielsen is deep and abiding.

Bersven Anderson

It may be of interest to note that one of the Haugeans from Maalselven was the pioneer Bersven Anderson. He was born in 1821, became a lay preacher in 1837, served as colporteur (bibelbud) in 1874, emigrated to America in 1876, and was ordained to the ministry in the Hauge Synod in 1878.

His mother was very delicate in health, and died soon after Bersven was born. Consequently he came

to this world so deplorably small and ill that no one
expected him to live.   His was an emergency baptism
performed at home, and the Christians prayed God
to be merciful to the poor little child and take him
home together with his mother.   On the day of the

BERSVEN ANDERSON

funeral they postponed the burial till long past the
appointed hour, since it seemed that little Bersven
was breathing his last, and there was a place waiting
for him on mother's arm in the coffin.   In spite of
this, at the time of his death Bersven Anderson was
the oldest Norwegian Lutheran pastor in America.

His father was very poor, and Bersven was taken into the home of a childless couple near by, and there spent his childhood.

After coming to America, his field of work was, for a period of 18 years, the entire Red River Valley. Somewhat regularly he preached at 20 different places of worship. As a rule he went a-foot to all these places.

He was the first and for many years the sole editor of the inner-mission paper: "Vidnesbyrd fra Broder-kredsen."

This paper is still serving the cause of lay preaching and has a large circle of readers.

At the age of 73 he went to Alberta, Can., where his countrymen at that time began to settle, and was for many years the only Norwegian Lutheran pastor in the whole province.

He died in the summer of 1917, having served continuously four-score years as a preacher of the Gospel.

The following tribute is paid to Bersven Anderson in "Fra Norges Kristenliv" (Kristiania, 1918): "He was a highly gifted and respected man; certainly one of the most remarkable of those whom Lutherstiftelsen has had in its service." His brother, Peter Andersen Moen, also a Haugean, served for a number of years as a member of the Storthing.

His son, P. B. Anderson, is a member of the church council of the Norwegian Lutheran Church, being the lay representative of the Canada district.

Nils Thorbjørnsen Ylvisaker

N. T. YLVISAKER

Another lay-preacher of considerable note, who for many
years was active as a religious
worker in Norway, and afterward
came to this country and was ordained to the ministry by the
Norwegian Evangelical Lutheran
Synod of America, was Nils Thor-
bjørnsen Ylvisaker. He was born
in Sogndal, Norway, in 1832. As
a young man of about sixteen he was awakened
to a conscious Christian life. This important change
of his life was brought about during an illness caused
by an unfortunate accident. While he was ill, several
Christian friends from the Haugean circles visited
him, among whom especially one of his comrades by
the name of Atle is mentioned. At the same time
he was diligently reading the writings of the church
fathers, especially "True Christianity", by Johan
Arndt.

During his spiritual struggles, which culminated in
"peace with God through a good conscience", he "obtained personal knowledge of what he later should
go out in the world to preach unto thousands of
souls." In 1850 he was made school teacher of his
home district. As such he met regularly with the
Christians for meditation and prayer. Presently he
also conducted meetings himself, as a rule on Sun-
days. At such meetings he would read a sermon from
a "postil," after which he catechised the children, and,
finally, "very zealously admonished those present to

repent and believe the Gospel. This was the beginning of his long career as a gifted lay preacher."

From 1855 to 1860 Ylvisaker travelled in the interest of temperance, at the same time also conducting religious meetings. From 1861 to 1868 he served
as emissary for "Det Norske Missionsselskab".

He had repeatedly been asked by friends to come
to America and take up church work here. In 1868
a regular call was extended to him, which he accepted
and became pastor of a church of the Norwegian Lutheran Synod in Red Wing, Minnesota, at the same
time serving congregations in the vicinity. Shortly
afterwards he preached the Gospel to his countrymen
in Minneapolis, and became the founder of Our
Savior's Norwegian Lutheran Church, now one of the
strongest Lutheran congregations of this city, the
metropolis of the Northwest. But his services in this
country came to an abrupt close by his death, April
16th, 1877.

Ylvisaker is described as a very able and eloquent
speaker, presenting a clear and earnest message of
salvation through grace alone. His true Haugean
view on vital points is brought to light especially
through his writings. Besides articles in religious
papers and magazines, several private correspondences
from his hand were published in "Ev. Luth. Kirketidende". From one of these we quote the following:

> "Oh, how true it is, what the singer declares:
> 'Det koster mer end man fra først betænker
> At være tro i det som Gud os skjænker.'
> (It costs more than one at first bethinks
> To be a faithful steward of what God gives.)

"Yes, it **costs,** for flesh and blood, to be followers
and soldiers of our Lord Jesus Christ, on earth. It

costs to pray at all opportune times, never tiring.
Grace abundantly is needed, which at all times must
be appropriated, in order to dwell among "wolves",
the devil and an evil world, at the same time retain-
ing the spiritual attitude of the Lamb, our dear Savior.
Yes, it costs diligence to walk on earth and live in
Heaven; for it is not enough that we once put our
hand to the plough, but it must never be taken there-
from; again, it is not enough that we once have set
our feet in the path of peace —not enough once to
have sworn one's self to the banner of Christ, taken
to the sword and viewed the goal. No, all this a soul
may have experienced and—oh, serious thought—still
forever lose the much longed for Zion Home, and thus
become a prey to the foe of souls. . . . May the Lord
help us to walk worthy of the call wherewith we are
called, so that we finally may greet the sweet wounds
of Christ. There shall the Lord wipe away all tears
from our eyes. Oh, what a moment!"

Ylvisaker repeatedly quoted hymns composed by
Haugeans, among them the one by Erik Venjum,
which elsewhere within these pages is given in full.

Three of Nels Ylvisaker's sons entered the ministry, all of them rendering distinguished service in the
Church. Ivar Ylvisaker is now the district president
of the North Dakota district of the Norwegian Lutheran Church. Professor Dr. Johannes Ylvisaker,
who for nearly 40 years was professor of theology
at Luther Seminary of the Norwegian Evangelical
Lutheran Synod, was a younger brother of Nils Ylvisaker.

*   *   *

But it is necessary to limit ourselves. To write
of the Haugeans in this country and the work that

they accomplished, would require a book by itself, and it certainly should furnish interesting reading.

We shall confine ourselves to mention one more Haugean in Norway, who in spirit was of the old, true type, but who belonged to the awakening in the sixties and who, for that reason, naturally leads us up to the second period of the Haugean movement.

Ommund Kallem

On Tuesday, June 28, 1904, seventy-six years of age, Ommund Kallem departed this life. These were the words he spoke to one of his most confidential friends just before his death: "Now I want to go home. I want to go to the great mansion which has been given me. My wife will come later. Tell the brethren that I die in the faith I have confessed."

OMMUND KALLEM

Ommund's parents lived in Etne, to which place they had moved shortly before his birth. When Ommund grew up he took to horse trading, and the life he led was naturally no better than the run of those engaged in this work at that time. Drunken revelry was very common. When under the influence of drink, Ommund (as well as others of his kind) gave vent to his pentup feelings in horrifying yells, such as one might imagine the Vikings used on their marauding expeditions. His was a reckless and untamed disposition.

But a strong religious awakening in Etne and other neighboring districts had begun. The prayers

of the little circle of Christians were answered. And
during this awakening the grace of God wrought a
miracle in Kallem's heart; he became a meek and
humble man. He had been deeply moved and thoroughly awakened.

But to give expression to what he had experienced
seemed impossible to him. Nothing would come of
him, men thought; he seemed to have no talents. It
is true that when a few Christians came together at
some friend's home, they might ask Kallem to say
grace at the table, but as to his participating further
in Christian activity, it was not to be thought of. It
must, of course, be mentioned that his knowledge was
very limited. He called all higher institutions of learn-
ing the "synagogues of Satan," and criticized a school
teacher very severely for story-telling. The school-
master had informed him that he taught the little children stories from the Bible; and "stories" to one who
had been converted from the life of a horse trader
were, to say the least, odious. But this was during
the years following immediately upon conversion. He
later acknowledged that his views had been narrow.

But time brought forth his latent talents. About
10 years after his conversion a mighty spiritual awakening passed over the districts of Ryfylke and Jæder-
en. One of the results of this awakening was the
founding of the inner mission society of these districts.
It was in this society that Kallem labored during the
remaining twenty-eight years of his life. He was in
active service from 4 to 5 months each year; the rest
of the year he spent in retirement on his little farm.
That these were months of study and prayer was
evidenced by the strong, fresh, living, yet simple message he brought to the people. His was a powerful,

not a polished language. He bore the sword of God to give battle, never for the sake of display.

Kallem was also a leading figure in the organization called "Stølesamling"—an organization dating its birth from the little prayer meetings of a few enthused Christians, held on the mountain between northeastern Ryfylke and Søndhordland. This organization accomplished untold good. It was while preparing for a meeting of "Stølesamling" that death came to Kallem, and that he uttered the words mentioned above. The words of sorrow as well as the words of appreciation expressed by many men, both lay and learned, told plainly of the deep love which the Christians cherished for this consecrated man of God.

Gisle Johnson

Concerning Prof. Gisle Johnson we quote Pastor Odland in "Fra Norges Kristenliv": "In attempting to sketch the character of Prof. Johnson, and in calling to mind his lovely personality, that which first and above all arrests our attention is his quiet, gentle and unimposing walk. This little man with the slender frame was to that degree modest and unpretending, that we cannot recall ever having known his like in this respect. He also prized a quiet and simple life. Much persuasion was required to get him to appear in public. Even when, in the vigor of youth, he appeared as the zealous preacher of repentance, he was moved to act only by the urgent call from others. . . . He was a man of wisdom and love, and possessed a soul-winning loveliness and deep earnestness, which made it possible for him to guide and comfort as few others could do. Therefore he was met with the most devoted attachment and the most respectful

gratitude from all who came in touch with him. A
large number of spiritually interested people, both lay
and learned, sought advice from him on questions per-
taining to the Kingdom of God.

"Cheerful joy was not the prominent characteristic
of this quiet and humble man, but rather a concealed
peace and happiness combined with a deep serious-

GISLE JOHNSON

ness, void of all pretense, which gave him an influence
greater than he was aware of. He was a man of few
words; and it is claimed by those who knew him well
that a harsh and bitter word never fell from his lips.
In his home many a meeting was held. The friends
of the inner missions often met there for the purpose
of mutual edification; there the board for inner missions met to discuss problems relating to their work;
and almost every morning, especially in the winter
time, poor and needy came to this home, and, after

receiving bodily nourishment, joined in the morning devotion.

"Johnson was a man of exceptional talents; he had a keen mind, a remarkable memory and distinguished powers in reasoning. On the other hand he did not so much appreciate art and esthetics. The want of due appreciation and the severe judgment on the one hand, and the warm, unmixed gratitude and devotion on the other — all of this Johnson bore with humility.

"Unnoticed and through deep self-examination, and under the guidance of his teacher, Chr. Thistedal, partly also under that of the great revivalist, Lammers, but especially under that of the Danish author, Søren Kierkegaard, he became a living Christian. Devoted to truth and wholehearted as Johnson was, he became as a Christian and as a preacher a man who did not compromise. It was the necessity of repentance and conversion which, with fiery zeal, pervaded his speech. Thus the young, learned theologian became an instrument toward an awakening within the Church of Norway." The awakening through Johnson, however, found its fructifying soil in the awakening through Hauge. It was not a new movement, but a continuation and enlargement upon the work by Hauge and his immediate followers.

A comparison of Hauge and Johnson brings to light immediately their many resemblances, and the close relation between the movements inaugurated by them. Both were by nature religiously inclined and introspective. Both came into conscious relation with God through an awakening. Both were impelled by a divine call to witness before their fellowmen, even though they were not ordained to the office of the ministry. The Christian life of both bore the deep imprint of seriousness with strong emphasis on self-denial. Both recognized unconditionally the authority of the Word of God and the Lutheran confessions; they cherished the deepest respect for law and order, of divine or of human origin. Both exercised a far-reaching influence, not only through public testimony by tongue and pen, but just as much through personal influence by private conversation by word of mouth, and by extensive private correspondence.

Both had their immediate followers — Hauge especially laymen, Johnson especially theologians — who continued and extended the work of the masters. Johnson, however, exercised the peculiar influence of bridging the chasm between clergy and laity — a work of most vital interest to the Christian church. The accusation was made against Hauge and Johnson — and therefore also against the movements which they inaugurated — that they represented the dark and gloomy type of Christianity ("den sure og svarte kristendom"). Hauge's accusers were the rationalists; Johnson's, mainly the followers of Grundtvig, but also some ultra-conservatives. Because they stressed so emphatically Christian self-denial, and for this reason rejected the so-called adiaphora, as, for example, amusements, they were branded as legalistic and censorious. Johnson excelled in keenness of mind and logical thinking. His splendid education, in contrast to that of Hauge's, may in part account for this. But Hauge undoubtedly took the lead in practical insight and private conversation. Both were endowed with talents above the ordinary. Another resemblance was, that neither of them showed much appreciation for the fine arts, and also undeniably exercised influence upon their immediate followers toward an under-valuation of the same. It should be mentioned, however, that this influence, as far as we can see, was not exercised consciously; but it was nevertheless true, probably more so of Hauge than of Johnson.

Peter Lorentzen Haerem

PETER LORENTZEN HAEREM

In order the better to acquaint ourselves with the character of the awakening through Johnson, we shall discuss briefly the life and work of one of his followers, Peter Lorentzen Haerem, the founder of the Christian young people's movement in Norway. Concerning his relations to Johnson it has been said that his attachment to his teacher was as the intense love and respectful devotion of a child, and Pastor Th. Klavenes declares that Haerem was the worthiest representative of the awakening in the fifties and sixties.

Through his grandmother, and particularly through his mother, Ragnhild Haerem, he had come in direct touch with Haugeanism. At the meetings held in Stavanger by the Haugeans, his mother was deeply impressed by the message of these laymen, especially by that of Haugvaldstad. She was also a frequent visitor to the chapel of the Moravian Brethren (brødrene) in Stavanger, where she received help and guidance which led to liberty in Christ, and assurance. Every morning her first act was in solitude to kneel and pray. The burden of her prayer was for her children, but she also taught them to pray, and early instructed them in the Word of God. She was well acquainted with the devotional writings of the Lutheran Church, and often read "Luther's Postil". The children loved their mother dearly; Peter never tired of relating how much he owed her. Upon leaving his home to go to the university, he turned at the threshold and said: "Mother, bless me!" The blessing was given, as well as received, with tears, whereupon he set forth on his short but richly blessed pilgrimage.

About the time of his confirmation his spiritual life awoke to consciousness. At the university he formed a Christian circle of fellow students, gathered them for regular seasons of prayer, awakened interest among them for missions — especially the mission for Israel, and gathered means from them for this purpose. After he had become a theological student he formed circles for Bible study and also held devotional meetings in the suburbs of the city. Oftentimes, upon returning from these meetings, he was seen in company with a band of men and women who pressed about him in order to continue the discussion. Only once in a while did he participate in the discussions of the theological society at the university; namely, when questions of a practical nature were debated, e. g., the adiaphora, or the interpretation of the fourteenth article of the Augsburg Confession, the very questions of vital interest to a Haugean.

While yet a theological student, he was made associate editor of "Missionsblad for Israel". Haerem's mother had often said: "He who would accomplish something for God worth while, must begin with the children and the young." For this very reason, in 1867 he invited a number of boys from the street into his study room for a devotional gathering. Out of

this originated the Norwegian young men's societies (ynglingeforeninger). Later he founded "Studenterhjemmet" (home for students), toward the establishment of which he received large gifts from an
English lady and also from the Norwegian capitalist
Sven Foyn. In 1870 Haerem became the editor of
"Maanedstidende for den indre mission", and was also
elected secretary of Lutherstiftelsen, an organization
for inner missions. In the interest of missions he
made several trips abroad. In 1870 he was in Berlin,
where he attended a general conference in the interest of Jewish missions. From Berlin he went to London, where he attended the so-called "May meetings"
— annual meetings held by the various Christian activities which have their headquarters in London. At
one of these meetings he had the privilege of address-
ing the assembly. He related about Lutherstiftelsen
and its activities, and thereby gained many warm
friends for this movement, both in England and Scot-
land. In 1869 Haerem became editor-in-chief of "Fæ-
drelandet", a paper discussing politics in the light of
Christianity, and dominated by Christian principles.
Later he, together with others, also published "Den
Norske Arbeider", an organ for the laboring man, and
"Hjemmet," a paper devoted to the interests of the
home. It was his plan, as far as possible, to make
the press serve the cause of God. The work con-
nected with these publications, however, did not pre-
vent him from travelling extensively, both in Norway
and abroad, in the interests of Lutherstiftelsen, home
and foreign missions, and the Christian young people's societies. It was chiefly through his initiative
that the mission ship named "Hans Nielsen Hauge"
was bought, in 1871. In the prow of the ship was a

life-size figure of the renowned layman for whom the
ship was christened, and the hand of which pointed
to an open Bible. The income resulting from the oper-
ation of this ship was turned over to Lutherstiftelsen
and the seamen's mission (sømandsmissionen) until
1886, when it was sold.

After fifteen years of uninterrupted, strenuous
work, his otherwise strong constitution finally gave

THE MISSION SHIP "HANS NIELSEN HAUGE"

way. His last trip was to Drammen, from which place
he returned sick unto death. Friday, March 15th,
1878 — when only thirty-eight years old — he died
peacefully, with firm faith in his Savior. The spacious
Trinity Church was far too small for the great multitude of sorrowing friends. A memorial service was
held at Studenterhjemmet, where Pastor Storjohann
and Prof. Fr. Petersen spoke. Prof. Gisle Johnson
spoke at a similar service in Hausmannsgaten's Chapel (bedehus). The poet, Jonas Lie, composed a can-
tata for the occasion, which was sung at the church.

One of the most efficient servants of the Church of Norway and one of the most prominent citizens of the country, had ceased from his labors and entered into the eternal rest.

He was often called a pietist, and in the right sense of the word he was a pietist. Some would maintain that he was not, strictly speaking, a Haugean. It is true that he cherished ideas which the Haugeans of the old type did not emphasize, as, for instance, the work for and among the young people. But he was in hearty sympathy with the awakening inaugurated by Hauge and Johnson, and was held in high esteem by the Haugeans. They certainly looked upon him as one of their own. Himself a layman, he staunchly defended the right of preaching by the laity.

C. M. Eckhoff

Pastor C. M. Eckhoff is another striking type of the awakening by Gisle Johnson.

A sketch of his work as pastor in Sunnelven, from 1867, is of unusual interest to us, because it brings to light very clearly how the men actuated by the spirit of this awakening conducted themselves as spiritual leaders in the church. The people of his parish are described as "deeply interested in religious questions." Outwardly they "lived an ordinary moral life, willingly aiding each other, being especially kind and charitable toward the poor and needy. They were regular in their attendance at family worship. Many considered this to be sufficient unto salvation; but others, again, had a sense, deep in their souls, that something was still lacking."

Pastor Eckhoff's first sermons caused a stir among the people. There was something new about his preaching. They were accustomed to able preachers, who had presented to the people the way of truth clearly and forcibly. The people were strongly impressed by their message. It was the good old Gospel they preached. Eckhoff, too, preached the old Gospel, and yet there was, as stated, something new about his message. His sermons were personal appeals. The Word of God penetrated deeply into the very heart, and made the hearers feel their individual responsibility. The call was sounded for a personal giving of account before God.

It was, moreover, strongly emphasized that such a personal meeting with God should be sought without delay, for it might become too late.

Another matter that caused considerable comment was, that Pastor Eckhoff desired a personal interview with every communicant. Some received great benefit from this interview, while others resented it. It also happened that the pastor advised certain individuals against partaking of the Lord's Supper. Then he began holding religious meetings in the various homes and in school houses. He desired to reach the people and to learn to know their way of thinking. In his prayers, publicly as well as privately, he asked for an awakening among his flock. It came in the spring of 1868. First in Geiranger, then in Sunnelven. People came to him in private to speak to him as their pastor about the condition of their souls. They confessed their sins and asked for guidance and intercession. All this caused the pastor to rejoice and praise God. He had prayed for it, he said, and had also felt assured that it would come, but did not expect it to come so soon.

Many were those who found peace with God.

These at once began to speak to their friends and
comrades, which in turn caused the awakening to
spread. But now the opposition was also aroused.
Some declared the movement to be only, or mainly,
an outgrowth of spiritual arrogance and fanaticism.
This, however, gave new and added force to the
movement, and after a while the opposition died
away; and some of those who at first looked askance
at the movement later became its warmest and most
faithful friends.

Eckhoff had not only the gift of awakening, but
he also had in an eminent degree the power of spiritual leadership. "The awakened met frequently for
the purpose of studying the Bible and discussing
spiritual questions and pray." One who partici-
pated in these meetings declares: "Ah, these were
blessed meetings! The people were led into the Word,
and into the experiences of other Christians. Questions were brought up and answered. In leaving the
meetings, one always felt that it was good to have
been there. The Christians were one heart and one
hand. They did not criticize each other, but rather
directed, prayed for and loved one another."

Pastor Eckhoff gladly received lay preachers, pref-
erably those sent by the board of missions. In 1868
he was instrumental in bringing about the organization of a mission society within his district. At a
general meeting of Lutherstiftelsen, held at Hjørund-
fjord, in 1871, a rather spirited debate arose obout the
rights and privileges of inner missions. In this debate
Eckhoff stood alone among the ministers present in de-
fending the cause of Lutherstiftelsen and its work.
It was a severe test of his faith in its cause, and his
love for it, but he came through the test unscathed.

The Christian laymen ever afterwards remembered
him because of the services he rendered, particularly
at that time.

Andreas Hauge

A mention of Andreas Hauge, the son of the famous lay preacher, will be in order. After having fin-
ished his theological training at the university, in
1832, he served in the capacity of teacher for some
years. Only 26 years old he was elected president of
the Christiania Mission Society, and as such was chiefly instrumental in bringing about the consolidation of
the various mission societies of eastern and western
Norway. From 1846 to 1854 he edited "Norsk Mis-
sionstidende." From 1850 to 1852 he was the secretary of the Norwegian Mission Society (Det Norske
Missionsselskap), and in this capacity he traveled extensively at home and abroad in order to become acquainted with missionary leaders and the best missionary methods. In 1857 he became pastor in Skien as
the successor of Pastor Lammers, the famous revivalist. Conditions in this congregation were not of the
best at that time; but he succeeded, by the grace of
God, to unify the various and conflicting elements,
and became instrumental in bringing signal blessings
to the church. From 1868 to 1892, the year of his
death, he also served as dean (provst) at Skien dean-
ery (provsti). Incessantly he labored for missions,
participating in district and general meetings, often
as chairman; whole-heartedly he took part in movements of reform within the church. In 1876 the gov-
ernment offered him the bishopric of Tromsø, which
he declined.

While the son thus represents the same spiritual

tendencies as his father, we also notice in him how
Haugeanism aligns itself with Christian life in Norway generally. As he at all times was a friend of the
"laymen", it is also significant that he married a
daughter of Pastor Gabriel Kjelland in Lyngdal, who
represented the "Brethren" movement in Norway.

II. HAUGEANISM

Fundamentals of Haugeanism

In the light of the preceding sketches it becomes comparatively easy to delineate the fundamentals of Haugeanism. Haugeanism is a product of religious awakening. Consequently the Haugeans were generally called the awakened (de vakte). For this reason also the burden of their message was a call to repentance and conversion. This presented the possibility of undervaluing the Sacraments, especially Baptism. Of this they were also actually accused. But history shows clearly that while the accusation might justly be made against some of the men of this movement, it does not apply to Haugeanism itself, nor to its leading exponents. The Haugeans prized very highly the means of grace and made diligent use of them, but they protested vigorously against their misuse; and not without cause. They warned against the use of the means of grace as a sleeping potion.

Because the Haugeans demanded a conscious transition in spiritual experience from death to life, and therefore hesitated in acknowledging others than the awakened as being Christians, they were accused of being censorious.

By 1799 the movement inaugurated by Hans Nielsen Hauge had gathered considerable momentum. This is evidenced by the fact that the press gave not

a little space to its consideration. The following ex-
cerpt from an anonymous contribution to one of the
dailies gives a fair idea of the general tone of the
attacks upon the Haugeans and Haugeanism:

"When these so-called saints go hither and thither,
and with whining voices, rolling eyes and long-faced
hypocrisy condemn reason and research in the sphere
of religion, clamor for blind faith, and pronounce re-
tribution, condemnation, devil and hell upon those
who would try all things and retain the good; . . .
when they, because of feebleness of mind, desire for
praise, or perhaps most often because of stupid con-
ceit and pride, in that they regard themselves as
alone worthy of heaven, denounce our country's clergy (with the exception of a very few) as false teach-
ers; when these same saints conduct themselves in
such wise, and by threats regarding the devil, condemnation and hell, preach such principles for salvation as are evidently in conflict both with reason and
with the teachings of our Lord Jesus and his apostles,
and thereby perplex, alarm and bring unhappiness to
the weak and simple-minded, though often good Christian, so that such a person with mind wrought up and
brooding, in spiritual distress and in inactivity, pines
away to meet an untimely death, or perhaps in dis-
traction of mind and fanaticism fancies himself called
by God or constrained by the Holy Spirit, and therefore sets out, frenzied and intoxicated by emotion, to
preach the same leaven unto others," etc. . . . . .
Having thus characterized the exponents of the movement, the writer concludes by "thanking the authorities for the provisions they have made toward ridding
us of these idlers". The "true worshippers of God
remain with God in their calling and do not roam at

random through the country, eating stolen bread, as do Hans Hauge and other swag-bellied idlers who feel no inclination to work." [1])

The injustice of the accusations is too apparent to need any refutation on our part. In the light of subsequent history the arraignment appears ridiculous.

Again, the Haugeans were accused of being legalistic, in part because in their preaching it was claimed that the Law was given a more prominent place than the Gospel, in part also because too much emphasis seemed to be placed upon seriousness and self-denial in Christian life. It is true that the accusations mentioned might justly be advanced against some of those who prided themselves upon being followers of Hauge, but we emphatically repeat that the Haugean movement itself and its standard bearers were not legalistic.

Let it be further admitted that in certain instances too great emphasis was placed upon things of minor importance, such as garments, gestures, and the like. There were homes where only religious books were tolerated; and there were parents who would not permit their children to read, even in school, any book not distinctively religious. The writer is personally acquainted with a man now living, who, while a boy of about fourteen, secretly came into possession of a geography — a book tabooed both by his father and the pastor. When he was found out he even received a whipping for his disobedience. The wearing of costly apparel and jewels, for instance, was almost invariably looked upon as indicating worldliness.

While they admittedly went too far in this respect, let it also be remembered that because of their serious view of life the influence of the Haugeans became so

_____

1. Translated from "Sambaandet," Bergen.

strong and lasting. Now, any great movement must
be judged not by its eccentricities, but by its central
truths; not by the more or less imperfect presenta-
tions of followers of the movement, but by its fundamentals. If Hauge and several of his followers did not
emphasize the atonement as strongly as might be desired, it was because of the fact that license in life and
conduct had been taken by those who made much ado
about grace and "the blood of the Lamb." He had seen
a great deal of this, for instance, among the Seeberg-
ians in his own community of Tune.[1] We must also
bear in mind that true Christians in those days were
few and far between; rationalism was rampant among
the clergy, and, as a consequence, the standard of
morality among the people was low. Hence the ever
recurring call to repentance, change of heart, and an
earnest, moral, self-denying life. Nevertheless, whenever the question of how to be saved was put to Hauge
and his followers, the answer was, invariably and without hesitation: By faith in Jesus Christ, our Savior,
only.

Haugeanism Compared with Orthodoxy and Pietism

It is to be noted, however, that the awakening of
Haugeanism was not altogether a new life in the
Church of Norway. Its root is to be found in the religious life prior to the time of Hauge, especially in
orthodoxy, and even more so in pietism. Thus, in

---

1. "Det er sandt, jeg lærte loven, men denne som tugte-
mester til Kristum, og som en troende Kristens daglige lev-
nets speil, at kjærlighed til Gud og næsten er den moralske
lovs fylde, og hvor dette tilsidesættes, føler jeg ikke megen
glæde ved de høie beraabelser om Blodbrudgom og hvile i
den Korsfæstedes aabne vunder, om de end med hine kvinder
noksaa meget græde over ham." (Hauge).

common with orthodoxy, it strongly emphasized the value and necessity of **pure doctrine, in accordance with the Word of God and the confessions of the Church.** It has even been urged against the movement that it went to the extreme in this respect. It is a matter of common knowledge that the followers of Hauge often have been opposed to changes from the old to anything new, such as revised editions of the Bible, new hymn books and new books of religious instruction for the young. Along these lines they were very conservative. Ole Gabriel Ueland once declared during a debate in the Storthing that Luther's Small Catechism and the national constitution were to the people of Norway "like the apple of the eye". When the followers of Grundtvig attempted to replace Pontoppidan's Explanation with one more to their own liking, their efforts were frustrated mainly by the followers of Hauge. While their position in this debate is to be commended, the methods often employed, together with harsh judgments at times pronounced on the opposition, cannot be approved. Like the champions of orthodoxy, the Haugeans have at all times maintained that the Word of God is the "sole rule and guide for faith, doctrine and practice." The relation of Haugeanism to pietism is equally obvious.[1] Both insist on a conscious change of heart; both emphasize earnestness and self-denial in the Christian life; both maintain the right and privilege of every Christian to testify before and about God;

1. "Hans (Hauges) bøger er ikke uttryk for en klar, ordnet tankegang; men de er utsprungne af en dyb religiøsitet og et strængt syn paa tilværelsen. Der var neppe nogen forfatter i hine aar som saaledes blev læst af almuen i Norge som Hauge. Folket kjendte de gamle andagtsbøger og var glade i dem, og igjennem Hauges skrifter klang den samme alvorlige religiøse grundtone som i hine" (Olaf Røst).

both lament the sinfulness of the "world", the spiritual distress of the church, and dead orthodoxy, and
protest against the false consolation sought by an outward participation in church services, especially partaking of the Lord's Supper without being rightly
prepared. The well known pietists called "Syvstjer-
nen", in their writing to the king, prophesied punish-
ments from God on the apostate church. In like man-
ner Hauge predicted that the prevailing corruption
and universal apostasy would provoke divine visita-
tions, that the Lord would strike the people with fire,
hunger, pestilence and war.

Another similarity is a firm belief in the right and
efficacy of the state to further Christian life and the
growth of the church by outward and legal means, in
spite of the fact that both movements in their beginning suffered by persecution from the state. To
Haugeanism these trials became a source of purifica-
tion and great blessings. The movements were not
to be man-made. After seven years of intense activity, Hauge was kept inactive for ten years—in prison.[1]

It seemed cruel. Many considered the cause lost.

---

1. An almost analogous example was that of John Bunyan
in England. Twelve years he languished within dingy prison
walls, because he had preached the Gospel to his fellow-men.
The first sentence pronounced upon him sounded like this:
"You shall be brought back to prison and remain there for
three months. If you, after that time, do not consent to go
to church and participate in the services (The State Church
of England), and also discontinue your preaching, you shall
be banished from the Kingdom. If you disobey this order,
and are found within the limits of this land (England) without special permission from the king, you shall hang by the
neck." To this Bunyan replied: "If I was liberated from the
prison today, I would, by the grace of God, preach the Gospel tomorrow."
It takes courageous men, fearless men, to be the standard-
bearers of truth.

Not so: the mills of God were grinding all the time.
Even when, in 1814, the state, after having made use
of Hauge for salt-making, returned him to prison, contrary to all rules of fairness, this, too, evidently served
God's purpose. The solitude imposed on Hauge at
this time was a good thing for him spiritually, as well
as for the movement. Thus the folly of men served
to enhance the glory of God.

Differences between Haugeanism and Pietism

On the other hand, the differences between the
two movements are evident. "The anti-pietistic element in Haugeanism consists in this, that it strongly
and fervently emphasizes Christian life in its activity
and strife, rather than in its rest and tranquillity. As
the pietists saw their ideal in being quiet, introspective, always looking upward, while their earthly tasks
were either distasteful or, at any rate, irksome and
wearisome; so the Haugeans were thoroughly practical men with a keen sense for the economical, a desire for activity which at times and in places went too
far, assuming a strong semblance to the worship of
mammon." Haugeans have, for this reason, assumed
leading positions along all lines of activity, from the
fisherman's boat to the house of parliament, and from
the time of the memorable gathering at Eidsvold down
to the present day.

National Traits Reflected in the Movement

It has been stated that the sense for the practical,
so peculiar to the Haugeans, as well as their emphasis
on the freedom of conscience, was a heritage from
rationalism. Plainly, this is a mistake. The true explanation is to be found in the view of life and Chris-

tianity which obtained among the Haugeans, together
with the fact that the leaders of the movement were
typical representatives of the national spirit of Norway.[1]

Repeal of the Conventicle Act of 1741

The low-churchly tendencies of the movement were
brought into prominence by the discussion as to the
right of laymen to preach the Word of God, and the
relation of such work to the churchly office of preach-

ERIK VENJUM   O. G. UELAND

ing. Pietism had formulated and established as law the
famous (or rather infamous) "Konventikelplakat" (ordinance) of Jan. 13, 1741. Rationalism interpreted it
to its own interest, and to the interest of intolerance;
Haugeanism suffered under it, fought it, and finally
succeeded in overthrowing it a century later, July 27,
1842. It was a long and bitter strife. In this contro-
versy the clergy of Norway almost unanimously op-

---

1. "Det maatte være noko med den sjælelege undergrunnen
i folket vaart, som gjorde, at Johnson og hans flok hadde
bettre tak paa folket med sin ljosrædde og livsrædde kristendom. Det høyrer med til huglyndet vaart, og det har røter
baade i natur og soga" (Høiskolebestyrer Lars Eskeland).

posed its revocation, and consequently it was a battle
royal between the clergy on one side and the laity,
supported by a few ministers, on the other. To the
famous Haugean, Ole Gabriel Ueland, the chieftain of
the peasant party and for many years the most influential personage in the Norwegian Storthing, be-
longs the honor of bringing this struggle to a happy
conclusion. Twice the question of the repeal of this
law was referred to the theological faculty, but this
body counselled against repealing the ordinance. Twice
the Storthing voted in favor of annulment, but both
times the king withheld his sanction. When the Storthing for the third time voted to abolish it, the resolu-
tion became law in spite of the king's veto.[1] It was a
hard struggle, but the cause of the laity triumphed.
And today there is hardly a man in the Norwegian
Lutheran Church, of Norway or anywhere else, who

---

1. Upon this occasion the well known Haugean, Erik
Venjum, composed the following hymn, which afterwards
became a favorite in Haugean circles:

> Hav tak, o Fader kjær,
> For saadan frihed er,
> At vi i fred kan tales ved
> Om det som hør til salighed.
> Ja takket være du
> Som bliver ved endnu
> At øse ned Aand, liv og fred
> I samlet menighed.
> O, underlig forborgne ting,
> Som saa opløfte kan vort sind
> Fra nød og stød
> Til liv og hvile sød.
> Min sjæl og aand, sind og forstand
> Sig svinger nu til Himlens land
> Og ønsker sig at komme did
> Til evig hvile blid.
>
> O naade og forsmag!
> Min sjæl blev let og glad.

would vote in favor of the ordinance in question. For the benefit of those of our readers who would be interested in the wording of this ordinance, we quote article 16, which especially deals with the points in question:

ART. 16. "It shall, furthermore, be absolutely prohibited for anyone, either a man or a woman, married or unmarried, to travel from place to place, alone or in company with others, for the purpose of awakening or edifying others, or to hold meetings. Each person shall remain in his own particular calling, live quietly, support himself honestly, eating his own bread; but people may visit with each other, in order to help and edify each other privately. No public gatherings must be allowed. But women, especially unmarried women, shall remain where they are, serve, work and edify themselves quietly and learn from others, as the Scriptures enjoin, and as it behooves their sex. Let them not imagine that they have any call to teach and preach. It shall be allowed, however, if they are fit for such work, and if anybody desires to engage them to teach their children at home, with the consent of the authorities and under the supervision of the minister, to read for the girls

Den byrden bar, alt dunkelt var,
Men nu blev veien klar.
Og verdens tanker svandt,
Nyt lys igjen oprandt,
Slig naadeløn gir os Guds Søn,
Helst under sang og bøn.
Har draaberne en saadan smag,
Hvad livets strøm i Salems stad!
Vi har tid rar,
Men kort, kjøb den, vær snar.
O, skulde vi ei hjertelig
Dog elske, ære, tjene dig.
Bevar vor sjæl, Immanuel,
Far, venner, far nu vel!

and to instruct them in Christianity and in branches
of knowledge that would properly benefit them. They
shall also be permitted, if they are gifted for it, and
if they are called to it, quietly to be of service to their
own sex, by way of teaching and edifying. But this
must not cause any stir, nor draw any gatherings." [1])

This monstrosity has now for some time rested
in the scrapheap of the past, but in perusing the pages
of its history, one is filled with disgust and indigna-
tion at the role played by the church dignitaries and
spiritual leaders at that time. The only consolation
is, that there were a few glorious exceptions to the
general rule.

Bishop J. C. Heuch

1. "Det skal fremdeles være aldeles forbuden, at nogen,
enten mandfolk eller kvinde, gifte eller ugifte, maa reise om-
kring alene eller med følgeskab fra et sted til et andet under
navn af at styrke og opvække andre, og der at anstille samlinger. Men enhver skal blive i det kald han er kaldet til,

Bishop J. C. Heuch is considered the most influential leader in the Church of Norway in modern times.

For a number of years Heuch attacked the preaching by laymen most fiercely—by mouth and pen—declaring such preaching to be contrary to the Word of God. But he later turned completely, and became an ardent friend and defender of the movement. His printed sermons are very valuable, and his apologetical book, "Mot strømmen," is of more than usual interest.

Extension of Privileges of Lay Preachers

BISHOP JAKOB SVERDRUP

By the repeal of the ordinance above mentioned, preaching by the laity was no longer a breach of the law, but it was permitted only in private houses or in chapels. At a later date Pastor Jakob Sverdrup, who shortly before his death was appointed bishop of the diocese of Bergen, assumed leadership of the movement which aimed at full recognition of this activity

leve stille, nære sig redelig og æde sit eget brød; hvorved det dog er uforment, at den ene kan besøge den anden, privat at opbygges af hverandre, men uden anhang at gjøre eller forsamlinger at antledige. Men kvinder især og ugifte skal blive paa deres sted, tjene, arbeide og derhos opbygge sig selv i stilhed og lære af andre som Skriften dem byder, og deres kjøn det sømmer, uden at indbilde sig noget kald til at lære og prædike. Dog er det dem uforment, om de dertil er skikkede, og nogen vil tilse dem sine børn hjemme i deres hus, da med øvrighedens samtykke og under presternes opsyn at læse for pigebørn og undervise dem baade i kristendom og i de for pigebørn fornødne og sømmelige videnskaber. Der er dennem og uforment med opbyggelse og undervisning, om de eragtes dertil at have nogen naadens gave, paa forlangende ved stille omgang at gaa andre og ældre af deres kjøn tilhaande. Dog skal nøie iagttages og paasees, at ingen samlinger eller opsigt derved forvoldes."

within the church. On August 22, 1888, he succeeded in getting enacted a law providing that laymen should be permitted to preach in churches, but only on the floor, not from the pulpit. This was as far as the law-makers would go at that time. In 1897, while Sverd-rup was church councillor in the cabinet, a law was passed permitting laymen to hold religious meetings in the churches when such meetings did not inter-fere with any regular services conducted by the pas-tor. The pulpit might be occupied by the speakers, and even the church bells could be used in calling the people together. The right of laymen to participate in regular services was granted by law as recently as Oct. 29, 1913. The question of laymen's participation shall be decided by the congregation, the pastor par-ticipating in the congregational meeting as a member.

A Theological Defense of Lay Preaching

PROF. DR. SIGURD V. ODLAND

Mention must here be made of Dr. Sigurd V. Odland who, as the learned theologian, very promi-nently championed the laymen's cause at this time. In 1891 he be-came Professor Gisle Johnson's successor as president of "Det Norsk-Lutherske Indremissions-selskap", serving in this capacity till 1911. In upholding the rights of lay preaching, he did not argue from the standpoint of "the universal priesthood of be-lievers," which had been customary up to this time, but rather from that of the gifts of grace (naadegaver) in the congregation. He argues that as a member of the body of Christ, each believer has his special gift. He who has the gift of "prophecy" (preaching), is thereby also called by God to use it to the edification of the congregation, and any man-made ordinance hindering or forbidding it should be considered null and void.

Concerning Church Polity

The low-churchly tendencies of Haugeanism have constantly manifested themselves in the discussion concerning church polity. The Haugeans have, without exception, ranged themselves with the friends of reform, who have demanded the right of the church to regulate its own affairs, and a simplification of the church ritual.

The Haugean view in this respect is given by Pastor Fredrik Müller in Volume 55 of "Luthersk Kirketidende", Christiania, in an article entitled "Of Clerical Vestments," from which we quote the following:

. . . "I have much affection and esteem for the older generation of clergymen whose very life and heart are in the Gospel of the crucified Christ; who continue in 'the foolishness of preaching' the sacrifice made on the cross, a doctrine often obscured and suppressed by the younger generation.

"But an extreme and remote symbology, by which one only mystifies one's self and others, I would that the proclaimers of the cross would leave to the ritualistic faction of the Anglican church, to the Roman Catholic and the Greek Orthodox churches, who deplorably obscure the clear Gospel and conceal it from the masses by means of their ritualistic flim-flam (væsen eller uvæsen); and rather content themselves with the impression which the simple testimony of sin and grace, conversion and faith in the Son of God, will always leave with our church-goers.

"It is indeed a question whether we clergymen, during these times of faint interest in symbols and marked appreciation of life's realities, would not accomplish more without gowns, surplices and chasubles.

"I doubt not in the least that these may have had their significance in an earlier age, when they enveloped the clergyman's person as well as the sacred rites which he performed in the congregation, with a certain nimbus; but I fear that these agencies now must be regarded as having outlived their usefulness, at any rate in respect to many whom our church should seek to win.

"The Socialists laugh at the clerical gown, old and young ladies rave about it, many of the friends of the inner mission (indremissionsfolket) are prejudiced against it. An able and active minister in the sight of God does not need to, nor does he wish to support his mandate and authority upon ornate robes of office, which serve to emphasize his position as a public functionary.

"Nor do the sacraments and the Word of God need these addenda. The means of grace have their power and sacredness in themselves for those who believe, and Holy Writ has given no command in regard to sacerdotal robes for the children of the New Covenant.

"Only to Israel has the Lord spoken of priestly vestments. Aaron's beautiful robes, all parts of which symbolized Christ's highpriestly work, were removed together with the high-priestship itself, being reflections only when Christ as the perfect high-priest en-

tered at once into the Holy Place, having obtained
eternal redemption for us.

"Why return to these shadows of symbolization,
and invent a priestly vesture respecting which God
has not given us the least indication, and keep up a
symbolical worship which the laity, no, not even the
minister, is able to comprehend and explain?"

While the above stated view may go somewhat
to the extreme, in the main, we think, the representa-
tion is fair and to the point.

Preaching by Women

Among witnesses for Christ called forth by the
Haugean awakening there have been not a few wom-
en. They also, without a doubt, were instrumental
in bringing about awakenings at various places. Of
these we may name Gunhild Høifjord, who often took
part in meetings in Drammen and Eker, "being very
highly esteemed." Og Sebille Sørum it is also stated
that "she was an instrument in the hand of God for the
awakening of many". Kristi Morken from Sogn is
well known as one who conducted meetings. When
Pastor Friis of Hafslo once examined her as to her
knowledge of Christianity, he afterwards declared that
she proved herself "to know as much about the subject as he himself did". MargretheVeum from Hafslo,
who, like Kristi Morken, was awakened by Hauge,
also held meetings, and was favorably known. In
Søndfjord lived Berthe Stenhovden; she, too, preached
the Word of God. Her sister, Randi Solem, is possibly the best known and the most prominent of them
all. Her grandson, Dean Solem, declares concerning
her that she possessed an unusual knowledge of the
Bible. Finally we make mere mention of Randi Gren-

dahl, from near Trondhjem, and Sara Ousten from
Østerdalen. While there is no word on record, so far
as we know, from Hauge or his prominent followers
respecting the right of women to preach, it is evident
that the participation of women in public prayer and
preaching was well known and appreciated.

Discipline

The Haugeans practised rigid discipline among
themselves, in spite of the fact that they founded no
organization. They did not accept an unknown traveling preacher without good recommendation from some
well known Christian, and they did not, as a rule, encourage a newly-awakened person to take active part
in the public exercises. It was deemed advisable that
those who would lead others must themselves have
some Christian experience obtained in the "school of
life".

III. SUMMARY

Haugeanism has maintained from the very first that every believer has the right publicly to testify concerning his faith, basing this contention on the teaching of the Word of God as to "the universal priesthood of believers." They had also demanded that this activity should be free within the congregation, that is, not under the control of the clerical office, but controlled either by the congregation itself or by the body of professing believers. For this purpose "Lutherstiftelsen" was organized, and later the various mission directorates. The high-churchly element either denied the right of preaching by laymen or demanded its control by the clerical office. Later the churchmen who favored the movement, as, for instance, Gisle Johnson, emphasized the so-called "principle of need". By this was meant that lay preaching would be in order only when there either was a dire need of more workers, or when the regular ministers were found to be unfit for their calling.

This view was based on the interpretation, at that time, of the Augsburg Confession, Art. 14. But this interpretation was more and more abandoned, and has now become obsolete. This strife is now at an end, God be praised! Lay preaching has become a recognized and permanent function in our Church. May it in the future, as it has been in the past, be a source of great blessing to our people!

No one will claim that Haugeanism has been without its shortcomings; in this respect it shares the fate of all similar movements. Neither do we mean to imply that the Haugeans have been saints "without spot or blemish." And yet it may with truth be stated, as has been so often stated by others, even by the most competent critics, that the Haugean awakening was **Light** and **Salt** to the Church and the people of Norway. And we repeat that among the Haugeans Norway has had in every respect its most intelligent, industrious and reliable sons and daughters. The results of the movement have not been confined within the boundaries of Norway. Its benign influence has also been felt in the neighboring countries, on heathen mission fields, and especially among us Norwegian Lutherans in America.

IV. PROSPECTS

The question arises: Can the movement maintain itself under the present conditions among us, as American Lutherans? The answer must be: Since Haugeanism represents such vital elements of true Christianity and a true view of life, it cannot possibly be limited in its operations by time or place. It is pointed out by some, however, as a matter of fact, that congregations which cease to use the Norwegian language in their services no longer have room for the work of laymen, in a Haugean sense. In view of this, some hold that, as our Church more and more becomes Americanized, Haugeanism will gradually disappear, because the soil is foreign to its nature. To this we reply: If the future developments verify the foregoing assertions, it will only prove that we need a new awakening, in order that we may preserve a precious heritage. And it should be a powerful incentive to Christians who have the well-being of our Church at heart, to pray God that He in His mercy will raise up prophets among us, who may go forth in the spirit and power of Hans Nielsen Hauge. Then let every one who believes in and cherishes what Haugeanism represents, diligently practise what he preaches and earnestly pray for the continuance of this precious element in our church life.

> "O Holy Ghost, to Thee, our Light,
> We cry by day, by night;
> Come, grant us of Thy light and power
> Our fathers had of yore,
> When Thy dear Church did stand
> A tree, deep-rooted, grand;
> Full-crowned with blossoms white as snow,
> With purple fruits aglow!"

www.ingramcontent.com/pod-product-compliance
Lightning Source LLC
Chambersburg PA
CBHW060157070426
42447CB00033B/2191